# KINGDOMS

*Deborah Keenan*

LAUREL
POETRY
COLLECTIVE

*Special gratitude and love to all the members of the Laurel Poetry Collective. Without the inspiration of these remarkable poets and artists, this collection would never have seen the light of day.*

© 2006 by Deborah Keenan

All rights reserved.

ISBN 0-9787973-1-0

Printed in the United States of America.

Published by Laurel Poetry Collective
1168 Laurel Avenue, St. Paul MN 55104

www.laurelpoetry.com

Book design by Sylvia Ruud

Library of Congress Cataloging-in-Publication Data

Keenan, Deborah.
    Kingdoms / Deborah Keenan.
    p. cm.
    ISBN 0-9787973-1-0 (alk. paper)
    I. Title.
    PS3561.E36K56 2006
    811'.54—dc22
                                                2006030114

CONTENTS

# The Bridge Poems

So Much Like a Beach After All     11

The Place of Old Order     12

And Then It Got Very Cool     13

Small Panacea and Lucky for Us     14

It Is Like a Reason     15

It Is Fair to Be Crossing     16

# Asleep and Dreaming inside the Song Asleep and Dreaming

Asleep and Dreaming inside the Song Asleep and Dreaming     19

The Boy I Quit For     21

Blue Heron     22

Travel     23

Nine Mile Creek // What Was Written There     24

Some Part of the Old Days     25

# Some Ways to Think about the Animals

Portrait of Soon    29

Backstory for ThunderCats    30

Some Ways to Think about the Animals    32

Deer    34

The Four Goldfinches and One Scarlet Tanager    35

# Kingdoms

Summer Wind in Autumn    39

July // The Right Hand Was a Medusa    40

August // No Rain    41

Two Sisters    42

If You Say Luck You Can't Say God    43

Not Getting Tired of the Earth    44

The Great Secret of Life    45

Between Now and Then    46

The Baby    48

ACKNOWLEDGMENTS

"Asleep and Dreaming inside the Song Asleep and Dreaming," published as a limited edition broadside commissioned by the author, created by book artist Regula Russelle for the occasion of the publication reading for Deborah Keenan, *Good Heart* (Milkweed Editions, 2003)

"August // No Rain," for Juliet Patterson, inspired by her poem, "June," published in *Digerati*, an anthology edited by Steve Mueske (Three Candles Press, 2006)

"The Baby," in *Water~Stone Review* 8 (2004) and in *Digerati* (Three Candles Press, 2006)

"Between Now and Then," commissioned by JoAnn Verburg for her installation at the Mill City Museum, *Between Now and Then, Minnesota* (photographic collage embedded in glass, steel frame on cement step)

"Blue Heron," to be published in Deborah Keenan, *Willow Room, Green Door: New and Selected Poems*, Milkweed Editions, 2007

"The Boy I Quit For," in *Bluefire* (Laurel Poetry Collective, 2005) and in *Digerati* (Three Candles Press, 2006)

"The Four Goldfinches and One Scarlet Tanager," commissioned by composer Sherry Wohlers Ladig, who was asked by womenperformhers to create a song cycle based on poems by a contemporary woman poet (this poem was performed along with "Butterfly Weed" and "The Noisiest Owl in North America," both published originally in Deborah Keenan, *Good Heart* [Milkweed Editions, 2003])

"If You Say Luck You Can't Say God," published in *Pulling for Good News* (Laurel Poetry Collective, 2004)

"July // The Right Hand was a Medusa," created in response to a poem by Juliet Patterson during a brief yet compelling collaboration and published in *Digerati* (Three Candles Press, 2006)

"Nine Mile Creek // What Was Written There," published in *Water~Stone Review* 8 (2004) and in *Digerati* (Three Candles Press, 2006)

"Not Getting Tired of the Earth," previously published in *Orion Magazine* (July 2004) and as a Laurel Poetry Collective broadside, limited edition designed and printed by book artist Georgia Greeley

"Portrait of Soon," in *dislocate*, online premiere issue (Fall, 2004) and reprinted in *Washington Square* (2005), *A View From the Loft* (Spring, 2006), and *Digerati* (Three Candles Press, 2006)

"Summer Wind in Autumn," in *Water~Stone Review* 8 (2004) and reprinted in *Bloomsbury Review* (2004)

"Two Sisters," in *Digerati* (Three Candles Press, 2006)

# The Bridge Poems

## So Much Like a Beach After All

Turn the alley sideways, running north to south.
Remove the houses on the south side of the alley.
Remove the years of cobblestones, tar, small stones.
See for quite a distance, knowing the water
Is just out of sight. Take a chair to the alley
Which is no longer an alley but a strip
Of ancient beach which your beautiful imagination
Has made. Sit in your chair and listen
For the waves.

# The Place of Old Order

Across the street the early summers
Three oriole nests swing
From the old linden trees.

If I walk toward them
I pass the grizzled cedar tree
That I understood as biblical.
Pass the line of French iris,
Pass the alert and waiting
Mailbox with its rusted
Red flag—the first flag
I understood. In the old
Order I was sent out
With a brillo pad to soften
The rusty edges, then
Painted the tiny rectangle.

Not that it was perfect.
Only that the chaos
Inside the home
Was faithfully balanced
With the extreme
Reliability of the natural
World waiting. I thought
I could pick and choose
From the old order,
Could impose such serenity
That all the days forward
Would be the western
View, the young orioles
Pushed from their cradles,
The flag lowered which would
Signal the letter that had to arrive
Had arrived.

## And Then It Got Very Cool

All the people who hate heat and summer
Came out of their houses.

All the people who hate cold and winter
Went into their homes.

The cast of characters changed
And newcomers to the planet
Searched in vain for their mothers,
Their fathers, brothers, sisters.

In the coolness of day and evening
Some of the best people found
Sanctuary.

In the coolness of day and evening
Some of the best people found
Their sense of exile had been misplaced.

The beautiful balance of the planet
Was celebrated by those interested
In this story.

## Small Panacea and Lucky for Us

Slight breath of wind
More wind and finally
The cloud over the cheery face
Of the sun, golden narcissist

One cigarette every three years
Or three cigarettes every one year

Love and only love, true love

The bridge in the distance
And the bridge close by

Constant misunderstanding
Of the real reasons

Being interested
In the motives of strangers

More wind, then if we're lucky
The rain falls down

Chance and luck set free
In what's left
Of wilderness

## It Is Like a Reason

*Oh, Yoko* plays softly in the din of the real
She walks softly through your imagination
Never having lost her center of gravity
Her angular beauty her craving for distance

The beach is waiting, though you forgot that
The summer, the love, the child, the stillness
Of early morning—one million things wait

The bridge waits benign in its sturdy indifference
Though you felt the darkness follow even as the world
Was turning, still, you walked softly into
Your own imagination, never lost
Your center of gravity     *Oh, Yoko*
*Hello*, you say, as she turns away

## It Is Fair to Be Crossing

Fair to choose the other side
And cross towards it.

Fair to cross over.

Fair to spend one hour
Of one's life considering
The meaning.

Fair to be humble
Yet take the chance.

Now you're on it
And you wonder:

What holds it in place
What if the wind
Picks up
Will the beloved
Be waiting
Will anyone else
Think it fair
That you have crossed
Will what you imagined
From steel and air
Be true
When you arrive
And go no further?

Asleep and Dreaming
inside the Song
Asleep and Dreaming

## Asleep and Dreaming inside the Song Asleep and Dreaming

*I've seen you laugh at nothing at all*
*I've seen you sadly weeping*
*The sweetest thing I ever saw*
*Was you asleep and dreaming*

Under grey granite they rest together
Under Utah skies
Over them all the force of weather
Over them the sighs

*I've seen you when your ship came in*
*And when your train was leaving*
*The sweetest thing I ever saw*
*Was you asleep and dreaming*

No ballad says it just the way
That I would have it said
No tombstone words will ever say
What either might have pled

*Well you may not be beautiful*
*But it's not for me to judge*
*I don't know if you're beautiful*
*Because I love you too much*

Because she found him beautiful
She gave her life to him
Because she found him beautiful
She shaped his life for him

Because he found her beautiful
He took her from her home
Because he found her beautiful
He was blinded to her home

It's not for me to judge their ruin
Not for me to save them
Standing by grey granite
Much too easy to love them

*I've seen you when your ship came in*
*And when your train was leaving*
*The sweetest thing I ever saw*
*Was you asleep and dreaming*

Stanzas in italic from Stephin Merritt's "Asleep and Dreaming," Magnetic Fields, Volume 2, *69 Love Songs*

## The Boy I Quit For

He's lovely, handsome, really.
When he arrived he had sunlight
White hair, rococo curls, gray/blue
Eyes oceanic and peering.

Now his hair's dark, straight, he's
Slender as reeds, slender as a mirror,
And smells of dense tobacco, of
Cigarette packs and ashtrays
From Toronto and Biscayne Bay.

When he arrived before dawn,
Serious and ours, I resolved to
Stop smoking—no other choice,
Really, with his skin smelling
Of angel and air, of soap and
Pure white cotton towels—no way
To keep the vice that kept me slim
And gave me such filtered pleasure.

Then I started again, not til he was
Two or so, then finally stopped, and
Sent him a letter. Dear J. I wrote,
You're the boy I quit for, in honor
Of life and love, wisdom and will power.
I quit for you, because it's right
That I should. I suffered the required
Length of time, and moved on, and
He moved on, moved out, and he's
Lovely, handsome, really, with
Gray/blue eyes and he moves
With grace through smoke
And I see him clearly though
I can barely see him.

## Blue Heron

We arrived carrying our usual human trouble, hoping to walk
Those troubles deep into the forest, hoping
To leave them there. Not as burden for the forest, knowing
All too well the forest and its beautiful indifference.

At the dam I looked left to a hidden curve of creek,
Joe looked right to the still water past the small island.
Blue Heron lifted from the curve, her wingspan almost
Touched us, and she landed past the island, bowed to eat.

Right after my mother died, eight years ago, I saw Blue Heron
In this small valley, I knew then my mother had left
Her exhausted body behind and slipped into this new
Winged disguise. I was happy for my mother's new life.

We've searched these eight years for one more sight
Of Blue Heron. And in our sorrows this day, three times
We saw her take flight, three times land, three times lean
Into shallow water for food and reflection. She's gone,

I said to Joe. We carried the sight of her back to our city,
Our hearts strangely stirred and strangely at peace,
Her extended wings visible against the green of spring.

# Travel

> People travel a long distance to be able to say: This reminds me of some other place—
> —#29, "Songs of Zion the Beautiful," Yehuda Amichai

Find the right place. First rule of travel.
Once found, live there.
When asked, say, "Yes, this reminds me
Of some other place. That is why I stay."

# Nine Mile Creek // What Was Written There

At the first curve of silt and sand:
Buddha slept here, and well.
And at the second, Jesus saves.
Do you? Jesus loves. Do you?
At the edge of the third swimming hole
We read: Kali makes it live and die.
Do you?

For fifty years my family's walked
In this small valley, always near
The banks, the creek water rust
And russet, metallic and gleaming.
For fifty years the secret springs
Help the watercress glow green
In all four seasons. Love, save,
Sleep, live and die. We answered
Yes to all, kept walking. The Blue
Heron who is really my dead mother
Come back to us, who is really a
Blue Heron, watches over us as
We read.

# Some Part of the Old Days

*for Sam, Cass, Gabe, William, Geoffrey, Susan, Cordelia, Joe, Molly, Brendan*

> Her porch light shines on anything that stands
> there in the yard with the wind in it.
> —Laura Jensen, "Her Porch Light"

Something I keep wanting to say to you ten.
Clichés abound. I send another birthday card
But want it understood it is about love.
And I know you all get it—it's about love.
And about your grandma Jinny's porch light,
How Dan and Larry and I let it light
The way home when young, how she put it on
For each one of you. Her ten. When I pass
The house now I am grateful the new owner
Believes in flowers. Still, I am shocked in my late
Middle age that your grandma Jinny is not there.
Wanting to make sure you ten know
She wanted every card game with you,
Every drawing you drew, every story
You wanted to tell. She wanted everything
Good for you ten. Her heart available,
And the light on.

Some Ways
to Think about
the Animals

## Portrait of Soon

> Perhaps the earth can teach us
> As when everything seems dead in winter
> And later proves to be alive.
> —Pablo Neruda, "Keeping Quiet"

Raccoons wrap their claws
In gauze, quiet as they cross
Linoleum, open the refrigerator,
Take only the fresh fruit,
The best vegetables.
Safely back in their winter
Forest they fling the gauze
Skyward, decorate the sleeping
Oaks, streamers calm and quiet.

The peony roots keep secret,
Avoid the crazy neighbor
With the roto-tiller, roots
Plunge straight down, commit
To another spring, to giant
White blooms streaked
With nature's quiet bloodlines.

The last one hundred tigers hold
Private meetings, plan the screaming
Deaths of zebras, decide to fight to stay
A part of this noisy planet, whomever
They must kill.

# Backstory for ThunderCats

Mythic, complex, the ThunderCats
Arrive from beyond any known galaxy,
Their kingdom the doomed planet
Thundera.

Their leader, wise Jaga, dead
Before they land,
Though his wisdom guides
Lion-O through five years
Of cartoon anarchy and order
Restored, week after week,
Wherever placed on
Network grids.

Mumm-ra is sustained
By his evil intentions,
His endless journey from
Dead to un-dead and back.

And Lion-O, though our
Assigned hero with sword
The size of a tree, wouldn't
Last an episode without
Tygra, Cheetara, Panthro, without
Those young dopes, WilyKat and WilyKit
To save and teach lessons to
Each cartoon week, without loyal Snarf,
Half dog/half cat, his magic powers
Seemingly dull when compared
To the others with better names.

There's so much backstory.
It's funny, and not, obsessive and right.

What I really remember is
The duplex, my first two children
Intent on the opening song,
The cry: Thunder Thunder Thunder ThunderCats! Ho!
Which I think of sometimes doing the six
Healing sounds in T'ai Chi, that *Ho!* Traveling
The jetstreams between cultures and centuries.
What I really remember is believing cats
Were better than dogs, and how happy I was
That people with power over cartoons agreed
With me. And I remember our cats, Max
And Rosie, padding silently around us,
Our good cats by day, who I'm sure
Protected Lion-O and fought
For the kingdom of cats each night
As we three slept.

## Some Ways to Think about the Animals

We needed porcupines. The handy quills for sewing and decorating ceremonial dress. After plucking the quills the body is just garbage, the soft meat not right for human guts so we toss it into the forest and the mice sleep in the dead fur, no quills to worry about now that the humans have set up their sewing kits. The mice watch the humans, and all the other animals, too. They meet to discuss only one thing: how to irritate the humans less. Humans don't want to eat them, don't want their fur, and still the humans want them dead.

From the forest floor, the prairie floor, mice watch bullets and arrows enter deer. See deer hung from branches, fur removed, meat removed, antlers removed, hooves removed—the humans seem to want every part of the deer except the deer itself. The mice don't like deer, either. Elephants and lions are irritated by mice, so when the humans slaughter elephants for tusks, cut lion heads off for wall ornaments, the mice don't really mind. One less stupid elephant with stone feet to stomp them, one less mangy lion slurping them down.

A time came when cranes got holy. People stopped shooting them. No more crane soup. The cranes cannot believe their utterly underserved luck. Artists rush in, draw crane at rest, crane in flight, crane as sacred alphabet, text for body and soul made from crane movement, crane stillness. The cranes are in a state of celebration for several hundred years, drunk on longevity and the peace only the lucky feel. Pelicans sick with bad nerves and envy keep lifting off in formation, but only some people love them, and no one thinks they are holy. Something about their formal flight brings men and women to the beaches with rifles. When they fall into the waves, no part of them is taken by the humans. The pelicans represent that other kind of human need, and the cranes thank their lucky stars for their long elegant legs, their delightful feathers that catch the wind in a way that pleases the humans.

It's too bad we need the hearts of leopards for courage, their fur for beauty, too bad we don't really need the bluebirds, useless and lovely. We are very busy getting rid of insects no one wants except crazed candy-makers, and when the bluebirds fly in mist released from low-flying planes only a few men building homes for bluebirds shed a tear.

It's too bad we can't agree to stop taking photographs of animals. It's too bad we can never figure out which animals to save, or why. At the pier a crow dive-bombed a tern. The crowd leaving port on the ferry cried out against the crow, one woman lifted her arm to show her partner what had happened, and the crow saw the glint of her diamond bracelet on the lifted wrist. The crow soared in, snapped it at the clasp and carried it away—his nest lined with precious jewels that pleased him. Only in brief ornamental images are the animals doing all right.

## Deer

They drink from the creek
By our bridge or around the curve.
Their drinking soundless, though
We see how the water moves
Down their throats. They drink
And move away with animal hush.

They run as we walk.
Years go by and still
We cannot find them.

There is a terrible sound,
Sometimes, as if antlers
Are tearing away against
Branches. As if they will
Cause themselves
Great harm to escape us.

## The Four Goldfinches and One Scarlet Tanager

At the eastern edge, bisque and caramel dunes
At the eastern edge, scrub oak and pine

Two mornings walking, the goldfinches
Making their inverted arcs, two by two

Shaping the yellow line of sun's fire
Shaping the under curves of daffodil cups

So quick, so brilliantly yellow and small
So sure as they stitched the oak and pine

Together with gold thread and tiny needles
Together they careened down the road

All four following the curve of the old
Pirate road and then gone, into the thicket

And staring in vain for them, bright morning
Companions, eyes adjusted to the shock

Of the perfect scarlet tanager, resting
On the tree they'd flown past in their escape

Darkest eye, deepest scarlet, stunned
That no one had been searching for him

Somewhere in the safety of the forest
At the edge of the dunes the four yellow

Birds repeated and repeated
Their beautiful geometry.

Kingdoms

## Summer Wind in Autumn

Lifted the long hair of weary mothers,
Turned the carpenter and his sawdust
Into a storm of work and beauty,
Knocked some babies from their strollers
But those babies were all right.

Summer wind had his set of memories,
Tarnished, rusted, gold and silver, too.
The martyrs framed in windows
Wept and bled for all of us,
But summer wind carried the tears,
The blood, the reasons, off to the kingdom
Of weather without meaning.

## July // The Right Hand Was a Medusa

*for Juliet*

The head, too. And the grief. And the children gone.

The door opened, and truly, a shaft of light intruded.
The door opened, and we should never have looked.

Curious women. We always were.
Someone told us it was a value.

Someone we didn't care for told us
To stop being curious so we knew we were right.

So, though we are held now, timeless and
Out of luck, out of time, we were in sunlight.

What Medusa meant changed and changed again.
Our luck and grief transformed, truly, we could
Imagine alchemy like that.

This took care of ten percent of the grief.

And that we were together, not alone.

## August // No Rain

Still summer, and on the steps of the museum
Poseurs and the arrogant gather in honor of art.

Your head was on fire—they couldn't let you in—
Those flames too weird and meaningful

Might touch off a golden storm inside the Monet.
Or not. You never, never know about art and money.

You never know about money and fire,
Their curious marriage, their rapture.

Nobody was drunk, though. I think the heat
Just makes people pray for rain that doesn't

Arrive. Nobody's drinking, nobody's cooking.
Too many people are forgetting they hate winter.

I'm not, though. I hate winter. And today,
I'm so uneasy standing near the rich.

I know it is not their fault they live under
The money tree, I know how hard it is for them

When the poor refuse to love art, refuse to pose
On the steps of the museum. Today

In the brilliant heat I would burn their money
And dip my brush into the cinders for art's sake.

## Two Sisters

There are two sisters.
One is more pleasant.
One wears skirts that swirl
Confectionary
And abrupt. One liked,
One not. Their value
Is, as Benjamin said,
Ivy wrapped a-
Round the ruin of
Their stories which we
Will never know. One
Is changing, one is
Not. One is not me,
One is not even
You. Sadly, this is
No riddle, and no
Tragedy that any
One might notice
Who pretends to care
About two sisters,
One gone on ahead,
One dressed and swirling.

# If You Say Luck You Can't Say God

You said God and luck and you can't.
Even on t.v. where people say anything
You can't.

And you said God and there's no such thing
As luck.
You shouldn't have said that either.

And you said luck, and blessed, and survive
And it was all right that you were speaking.

You others—someone like me will tear
Your mouths away from your faces.

You said God and luck and I shot out the t.v.
Screen and the glass was glass and shattered.

And you said God, no luck at all, and I
Attacked the outlet, the short black cord,
The lethal prongs.

Don't talk about God. Shut up.
And you, the one who said luck and blessed
And survive. You can shut up, too,
But you can keep your face, and your mouth
For kissing.

## Not Getting Tired of the Earth

He can go to the moon. And Mars, too.
Take his patronizing face, vicious voice,
His appalling definitions of loyalty,
He can go.

The rest of us, we need to not get tired
Of the earth. Need to care for parrots,
Even if we don't, revere sand, and buffalo,
Butterfly weed and dunes. We need to not
Get tired of the shattering beauty we live with,
Need to not get tired of wacky little city
Gardens, need to not be bored with
Starlings circling, the holy crows
Calling, the prairie grass replanted,
Blade by blade. No sleep! No sleep!

Or, at the very least, no sleeping
All at the same time. The ones who
Want to leave for Mars seem never
To sleep, yet seem unable to hear wrens
Arrive in spring, the last lion roaring
Out his furious, golden protest.

I won't get tired of the earth. Will
Love the moon from here, will
Rejoice when those who do not
Love the earth can only imagine
It from their new permanent homes
In the sky.

# The Great Secret of Life

*for Dorothy, Connie, and Jean*

It's T'ai Chi. I know enough to answer the riddle
In the first line. We four balance the Chi once a week
At Jean's, and the electric serenity surrounds and protects us
Before we head off to the somewhat ridiculous real world
That seems to still need us.

Some weeks doing *daughter on the mountain*, then
*Daughter in the valley* I think of my two girls. Usually,
Though, I just think of all girls—I think we four women
Are building something for girls as we make these shapes
In the air.

Some moves are so clearly based on the lives and skeletons
Of cranes and great blue herons—on a very good night
I am the great blue heron, almost lifting off my feet, surprised
I am not in flight.

Some nights any one of us might arrive with too much sorrow,
Too many burdens to shake, and any one of us might miss
A stance, *pull taffy* wrong, forget for a moment the shapes
And patterns our bodies carry deep in memory. The shock

Of T'ai Chi is that's ok—I fall from crane or heron back
Into my woman's body, Connie might be doing moves
In double-time, Dorothy pause to reclaim the count,

Jean keep *carrying the ball* to the east one
Too many times—all is forgiven in T'ai Chi. This

Feeling of forgiveness shocks—some nights it envelops
Me as I drive away, the music pounding in my car.
My friends and I make what can cure one night a week.
Lucky Jean, to fall asleep where we four have *push/pulled*
And shaped the air, air now softened, forgiving, healed.

## Between Now and Then

> *Art and nature...that's what lights it up*
> —Jean Valentine

The cottonwood tree was what mattered first to me.
Cottonwoods meant water close by, I could follow
The trees which led to the creek which led to the river.
And I did.

The prairie was what mattered first to me. How the wind
Moved the fields, how the wheat and prairie grasses
Lay down to let the wind pass by, rose up to hide
The wild turkeys, the frantic, focused field mice,
And me, not frantic, not focused, just a girl in the middle
Of the country.

The sun was what mattered first to me. We would drive
North to find my Swedish relatives, stop near open fields,
Throw down a blanket, eat our lunch and watch red-winged
Blackbirds race and spin in the ditches, the sun burning
Away the smell of my dad's cigarette smoke, my mom's
Low voice.

Summer was what mattered first to me. Freed from proving
My goodness each school day I would walk in the bed
Of the creek as farmland gave way to wildness. On lucky
Days the cotton would be floating and flying, turning
The ground white, or landing on the water, and the water
Would rush the cotton away. Better than snow, in that heat
The cotton would cover the world as I knew it, and no voice
Could reach me in that little valley.

Between then and now matters to me. This northern star
State where I have abided, my ancestors arriving in
New York harbor, making their way to Moorhead,
Living by the Red River, farming, running newspapers,
Building little cabins and tiny saunas,

Stealing away from their endless labor to linger
In summer sun for just a few days. And we would
Drive towards them, through hours and hours of
Silver gold fields, and it mattered to me.

But the first thing that mattered to me was the cottonwood
Tree, anchor and glory, shade and beauty, sign
Of water nearby, tree I could follow, then and now.

# The Baby

She had a brief and beautiful greed for milk, the color blue, for more milk and many late-night television shows. She was constantly luminous, showily glowish, when we carried her from the prairie to the west coast her glittering skin and eyes sustained and inspired us, though we were not pioneers.

The baby, born in winter, loves summer. The baby loves being warm, hot even. The baby lies facedown on a blue towel and dreams of reindeer who do not glow with radioactivity, dreams of lions.

And now the baby, in October, admits summer has ended. And now the baby hates us all for our powerlessness. Sick of our love, sick of being carried. Preferring her crib, her mobile of six Shetland ponies, spinning and neighing.

She was just a little wild, the baby. Her parents were a little too tame, so she got to be a little too wild. Not like a reindeer at all, much more like a tawny ragged lion. But small, a very small secretive kind of lion, with teeth that could hurt you. She was a small, dark gold lion right here on earth.

DEBORAH KEENAN is the author of six collections of poetry. Her newest, *Good Heart*, was published by Milkweed Editions in 2003, and is in its second printing. Keenan is a professor in Hamline University's Master of Fine Arts in Writing, and Master of Liberal Studies programs. She also teaches at The Loft, and privately. She is a founding member of the Laurel Poetry Collective, a group of twenty-two poets and book artists.

With her colleague and friend Roseann Lloyd, she edited *Looking For Home: Women Writing About Exile*. This multicultural anthology won the American Book Award in 1991. She has received two Bush Foundation Fellowships for her poetry, a Loft-McKnight Award of Distinction for her poetry, and a fellowship from the NEA. Deborah Keenan is married to Stephen Seidel, director of urban programs for Habitat for Humanity International. She has four children, one granddaughter, and lives in beautiful, mysterious St. Paul, Minnesota.

Her other collections are: *Household Wounds*, New Rivers Press; *One Angel Then*, designed and hand printed by Gaylord Schanilec—a first project of Midnight Paper Sales Press; *How We Missed Belgium*, jointly written with Jim Moore, and winner of a competition for collaborative texts from Milkweed Editions; *The Only Window That Counts*, New Rivers Press; and *Happiness*, CoffeeHouse Press. In 2007 Milkweed Editions will publish *Willow Room, Green Door: New and Selected Poems*.

## LAUREL POETRY COLLECTIVE

A gathering of twenty-two poets and graphic artists living in the Twin Cities area, the Laurel Poetry Collective is a collaboration dedicated to publishing beautiful and affordable books, chapbooks, and broadsides. Started in 2002, its four-year charter is to publish and celebrate, one by one, a book or chapbook by each of its twenty-one poet members. The Laurel members are: Lisa Ann Berg, Teresa Boyer, Annie Breitenbucher, Margot Fortunato Galt, Georgia A. Greeley, Ann Iverson, Mary L. Junge, Deborah Keenan, Joyce Kennedy, Ilze Kļaviņa Mueller, Yvette Nelson, Eileen O'Toole, Regula Russelle, Sylvia Ruud, Tom Ruud, Su Smallen, Susanna Styve, Suzanne Swanson, Nancy M. Walden, Lois Welshons, Pam Wynn, Nolan Zavoral.

For current information about the series—including broadsides, subscriptions, and single copy purchase—visit:

www.laurelpoetry.com

or write:

Laurel Poetry Collective
1168 Laurel Avenue
St. Paul, MN 55104


NORMANDALE COMMUNITY COLLEGE
LIBRARY
9700 FRANCE AVENUE SOUTH
BLOOMINGTON, MN 55431-4399